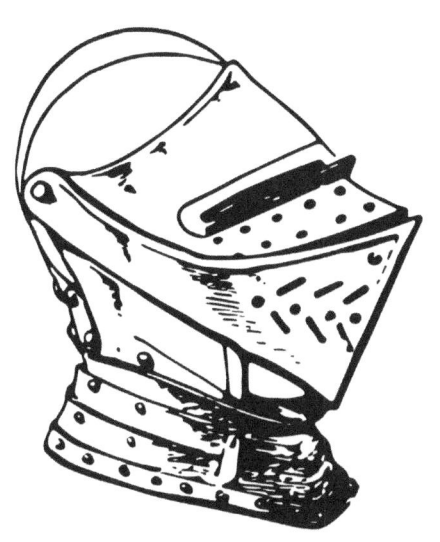

ALWAYS
READY

STEVEN R. MARTINS

ALWAYS
READY

STEVEN R. MARTINS

cántaro
publications

A PUBLISHING IMPRINT OF THE CÁNTARO INSTITUTE

cantaroinstitute.org

Always Ready

Published by Cántaro Publications, a publishing imprint of the Cántaro Institute, Jordan Station, Ontario, Canada

© 2022 by Cántaro Institute. All rights reserved. First published in 2021 as the first chapter to *Apologetics: Studies in Biblical Apologetics for a Christian Worldview*.

Except for brief quotations in critical publications or reviews, no part of this book may be reproduced in any manner without prior written consent from the publishers.

Unless otherwise indicated, Scripture quotations are from the ESV® Bible (The Holy Bible, English Standard Version®). Copyright © 2001 by Crossway, a publishing ministry of Good News Publishers. Used by permission. All rights reserved.

Illustrations sourced from Pixabay.com

For volume pricing, please contact
info@cantaroinstitute.org

Library & Archives Canada

ISBN: 978-1-7776633-6-0

Printed in the United States of America

TABLE OF CONTENTS

ONE   The Apologetic Mandate   **9**

TWO   An Exposition of 1 Peter 3:15   **17**

THREE   What is Apologetics?   **33**

FOUR   A Holistic Faith   **47**

FIVE   The Nature of Apologetics   **57**

SIX   Concluding Remarks   **71**

SCRIPTURE INDEX   **77**

"…but in your hearts honor Christ the Lord as holy, always being prepared to make a defense to anyone who asks you for a reason for the hope that is in you; yet do it with gentleness and respect"

– 1 Peter 3:15

CHAPTER 1

THE APOLOGETIC MANDATE

IT WAS THE EARLY fifth century AD, Rome had been sacked by the Visigoths, and the Roman pagan traditionalists, angry with the decline of the empire, came down with heavy criticism against the Christian church. What had happened? Not long since the church's founding in the book of Acts, Christianity became the predominant religious worldview of the Roman empire. It had even been adopted by the Roman state, dating back to the early fourth century AD, during the reign of Emperor Constantine I. This enmasse adoption resulted in such a potent change in the life of the empire that paganism took a back seat and become the belief of the minority. As historian Justo L. Gonzalez writes:

> The ancient religion [paganism] had no name, except those of the various gods. After the events of the fourth century, it was relegated to the most remote areas of the empire and... the word for *rustic*, ("*paganus*")... came to refer to those who followed the an-

cient, now rural, religion.[1]

The pagans believed, however, that as a result of abandoning the traditional Roman religion, the civilization's ill fate at the hands of the Visigoths was a punishment from the gods. With such livid and defamatory accusations, arising from pagans of all stripes, the Christian bishop St. Augustine of Hippo was compelled to write in response *The City of God*, a large tome that served both to console Christ-followers with the biblical promise of gospel victory and to refute the opponents of the one true Christian faith. As we look back today, *The City of God* has become a beautiful and classic masterpiece that portrays human history as a conflict namely between the earthly city (the city of man) and the city of God, a temporal conflict that is destined to end in ultimate victory for the latter. What Augustine wrote was ultimately an apologetic, and in many ways, he exemplified what

---

1. Justo L. Gonzalez, *The Story of Christianity, Vol. 1: The Early Church to the Dawn of the Reformation* (San Francisco, CA.: HarperOne, 2010), 142.

the biblical apologetic mandate entailed. I would even go as far as to say that *The City of God* effectively serves the modern church as a time tested and enduring blueprint for a comprehensive approach to Christian apologetics.

It cannot be denied that apologetics has become very popular in our day and age. In fact, most Christians now have an understanding as to what apologetics *is*, but what remains unclear to many is what the apologetic *mandate* entails. And there is a mandate, not an *independent* mandate from the Great Commission (Matt. 28:18-20), but rather one inseparably *tied* to it. Contrary to what has been the prevailing perspective in the twenty-first century church, the apologetic mandate is not a defense of our 'privatized' faith, that would be far too narrow or myopic – it also misunderstands the gospel. Instead, faithful to the cosmic nature and scope of the gospel, the apologetic mandate is a *holistic* defense of the Christian philosophy of life, that means "all-comprehensive", "all-encompassing", a "total system". It is not simply a defense of a few Christian doctrines, but a defense of the whole Christian worldview, a *world-and-life view.*

My objective for this publication is to make clear the *holistic* nature of our apologetic mandate by providing an exposition of 1 Peter 3:15, along with supporting scriptural passages that help us understand the apostolic instruction within the context of the gospel-centered mission of the church.

CHAPTER 2

AN EXPOSITION OF
1 PETER 3:15

WHEN CONSULTING the first epistle of Peter, it is important to first consider that this epistle was not written to a specific audience, not in the narrow sense, as say, Paul writing to the church in Corinth, or Ephesus, etc. Instead, from what we can understand from the text, Peter wrote his epistle sometime between AD 62 and 63 with a broad audience in mind, that is, the collective church, scattered throughout the Roman empire (1 Pet. 1:1-2).[2] He would not have been aware of the exact ethnic and social composition of his audience, but this much he did know, he was writing to both believing Jews and Gentiles, as is evident throughout the text (1 Pet. 1:18, 21; 2:6, 9, 11-12; 4:3-5; 5:13). And given how many more Gentiles there were than Jews in the church, the recipients of the epistle would have been predominantly Gentile.[3]

---

2. "Introduction to 1 Peter", *ESV.* Accessed August 12, 2019. https://www.esv.org/resources/esv-global-study-bible/introduction-to-1-peter/; J. Ramsey Michaels, *Word Biblical Commentary, Vol. 49: 1 Peter* (Waco, TX.: Word Books Publisher, 1988), xlv.

3. Ibid., xlvi.

It is with that in mind that we can then understand the text of 1 Peter 3:15 as apostolic instruction towards the *collective* church, not to an isolated community for an isolated event or circumstance. The text reads:

> ...but in your hearts honor Christ the Lord as holy, always being prepared to make a defense to anyone who asks you for a reason for the hope that is in you; yet do it with gentleness and respect...

Prior to expositing this verse, however, it is important to first consider the literary context surrounding Peter's instruction.

In the third chapter of 1 Peter, from verses 8 to 22, Peter provides instruction to the church as to how to live as Christ-followers in a hostile world. Having been forgiven of their sin, redeemed from their fallen condition, reconciled to God in Christ, and called to be the light and salt of the earth, the first-century Christ-follower would no doubt have clashed with the ways of the world, for no longer did they live as they once did before, in the futility and profanity of their sin. Instead, in Christ they were made a new creation, restored to their original righteousness by the gradual sanctification of their being through the power of the Spirit of God, and this produced inevitable fruit (Gal. 5:22-23). This *new* reality is not one experienced beforehand, and thus the apostles well understood that instruction was necessary in order for Christ-followers to live their lives in such a way that would glorify God in the midst of the world's fallenness.

The archbishop Robert Leighton, in his book *Commentary on First Peter*, expounds the purpose of not only this section but of the entire epistle:

> This excellent Epistle (full of evangelical doctrine and apostolical authority) is a brief, and yet very clear summary both of the consolations and instructions needful for the encouragement and direction of a Christian in his journey to Heaven, elevating his thoughts and desires to that happiness, and strengthening him against all opposition in

the way, both that of corruption within, and temptations and afflictions from without.[4]

It is in understanding this literary context that we can then proceed to the text to uncover its meaning, beginning with the opening words "but in your hearts honor Christ the Lord as holy". Contrary to what the popular perceptions may be of the "heart" in Scripture, which from the outset is certainly *not* the emotional aspect of man, nor is it the biological organ, Scripture regards the "heart" as the *root unity*, or center of the human person, equivalent to the concept of the soul.[5] The "heart" is the center of who we are, it

---

4. R. Leighton, *Commentary on First Peter* (Grand Rapids, MI.: Kregel, 1972), 9.; While Leighton has a bit of a retreatist bent – in that he interprets the Christian's journey as being heavenward, that is to say, that his final destination is 'heaven' as opposed to the redemption of the entire cosmos, where the renewed earth shall be our eternal home – he is nonetheless right in the general purpose of the epistle.

5. Joseph Boot, "Enlightened Hearts", *Ezra Institute for Contemporary Christianity*. Accessed June 10, 2017.

is the wellspring of life. It is thus in the root unity of the human person, or in the center of our being, that we are to "honor Christ the Lord as holy." However, the Greek text does not mean "to make holy", but rather to "acknowledge or declare to be holy", similar to the opening of the Lord's prayer (Matt. 6:9).[6] What Peter means to say is that, just as in the Old Testament, where God's people of Israel were to reflect the holiness of God to all the nations, Christians are to reflect the holiness of Jesus Christ through everything they do, the life expression of their confession that Jesus Christ is Lord.[7] This would include situations in

---

https://www.ezrainstitute.ca/resource-library/institute-minutes/enlightened-hearts/.

6. Michaels, *Word Biblical Commentary, Vol. 49: 1 Peter*, 187.

7. The sixteenth century reformer John Calvin writes that "it is the confession which flows from the heart alone which is acceptable to God, for unless faith dwells within, the tongue prattles in vain. It must therefore have its roots within us, so that it may afterwards bring forth the fruit of confession" in *Calvin's Commentaries: The Epistle of Paul the*

which Christians might find themselves in the midst of persecution, faced with inevitable "interrogations and threats" given the hostile conditions of their cultural missional context.[8] As scholar J. Ramsey Michaels affirms, "The task of a holy people is to make known to the world the Holy One who called them" (1 Pet. 1:15-16; cf. 2:9b).[9]

The next portion of the text reads "always being prepared to make a defense to anyone who asks you for a reason for the hope that is in you". Not only are Christians to reflect the holiness of Christ through all they do, they are also to be "always prepared", a readiness that can be likened to the constancy of loving one another as is likewise expected of the Christian.[10] Always prepared for what? To "make a defense", to give

Apostle to the Hebrews and The First and Second Epistles of St. Peter, trans. William B. Johnston (London, UK.: Oliver and Boyd, 1963), 290.

8. Michaels, *Word Biblical Commentary, Vol. 49: 1 Peter*, 187.

9. Ibid.

10. Ibid., 188.

an *apologia*, for "the hope that is in you", the hope that is in our hearts, in our root unity, in the center of our being.[11] The Greek word *apologia*, in the cultural setting of which this epistle was written, was used for a "formal defense in court against specific charges" (as for example Paul in Acts 22:1; 24:10; 25:8, 16; 26:1-2, 24; 2 Tim. 4:16).[12] As early as the late first century AD, Christians were accused of being atheists, in spite of the fact that they worshiped Jesus Christ as Lord, because they rejected the divinity of the Roman Emperor. Many Christians would have had to respond to such accusations, some even in a formal legal setting, however "legal" defenses in the strict sense of the term is not implied here.[13] What could instead be said is *any*

11. In *BDAG*, for example, *apologia*, is cited to mean: "the act of making a defense, gener. Of eagerness to defend oneself 2 Cor. 2:11. Of defending the gospel Phil 1:7, 16. Ready to make a defense to anyone 1 Pt 3:15." Cited in *BDAG*, 117.

12. Ibid.

13. Wayne A. Grudem, *Tyndale New Testament Commentaries: 1 Peter* (Downers Grove, IL.: IVP Academic, 2009), 161.

justification provided in an informal exchange, which could occur "between Christian and non-Christian at any time and under varied circumstances", this is the *apologia* that Peter had in mind.[14] To put it simply, Christians are to be ready in any circumstance – not just in formal exchanges – to give a well-reasoned defense for the hope that they have within them.

It is only natural that radically different living would prompt questions from those around us. If we notice a sudden change of behavior in our spouse or children, we may ask, what has produced such a change? Regardless as to whether such a change was a positive or negative one. The radical change that occurs in the life of the sinner, when he is drawn by the grace of God and touched by the transforming power of the Spirit, will inevitably prompt questions. Questions from those who are familiar, and questions from even those who are unfamiliar, who would otherwise expect certain cultural norms to be followed or

---

14. Michaels, *Word Biblical Commentary, Vol. 49: 1 Peter*, 188.

supported (i.e., cult worship, abortion, same-sex marriage, etc.). In light of who Christians are, contrasted with the natural man and the fallen world they live in, Peter views the church as continually "being 'placed on trial' every day" as she lives for Christ in a pagan, pluralist, and humanistic society.[15]

But what is this "hope" that Peter mentions? Clearly this "hope" is what prompts questions from others. This "hope" is what is expressed and manifested in the life of the Christian. This "hope" is what distinguishes the Christian from the natural, unregenerate man.[16] It is related to Christ, to the Christian's confession, to the heart and life change, but how might we articulate this "hope"?

This hope is none other than the holistic gospel of Jesus Christ, who has come not only to save man from his sin, but to also restore him to his rightful place and function, and to restore all of creation with him for

---

15. Ibid.

16. Grudem, *Tyndale New Testament Commentaries: 1 Peter*, 161.

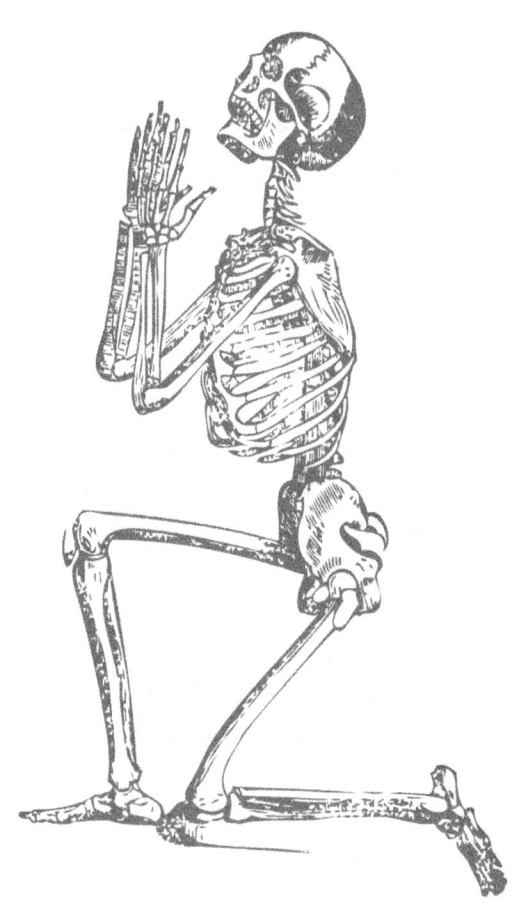

the glory of God. It is far more than just the rescue of the human "soul", it is the promised redemption of all things (Ps. 102:25-26; Isa. 11:6-9; 25:8; 65:17; Rom. 8:22-24; 1 Cor. 15:26, 54; 2 Pet. 3:10-13; Rev. 21). It is this "hope" that Christians are to provide a well-reasoned *apologia* for, but "with gentleness and respect".

What is meant by "gentleness" and "respect"? At first, we may perceive this to mean "gentle" and "respectful" in our speech towards all those who ask us about the hope within us, and that would not be wrong. However, there is something far deeper here that not only concerns our speech, but our relationship. Michaels comments that these words are to be understood as "an inward quality or attitude of mind (cf. 3:3-4), a profound acknowledgment of the power of God, and of one's own poverty and dependence on Him (cf. Matt. 5:5)."[17] This inward quality or attitude of mind is reflected in our relationships with other people. How so? If God alone saves, then we have

---

17. Michaels, *Word Biblical Commentary, Vol. 49: 1 Peter*, 189.

nothing in ourselves to boast of. If salvation comes by the grace of God, then our good deeds are nothing but worthless rags when they are performed for the sake of our salvation. To put it plainly, we neither have the power to save ourselves, nor a penny of righteousness in the bank to make us righteous, on the contrary, we are spiritually bankrupt and depraved sinners as long as we are apart from Christ. And even when we have been saved by His grace, that does not mean we can then go our own way after having been made right again, on the contrary, we need His sustaining grace, and we need the power of the Spirit to continue sanctifying us until we reach the perfection of our Lord Jesus Christ. We need the Triune God of Scripture on a daily basis, for every hour, every minute, every second. When we understand how wide and how deep the grace of God is, how can we not be gracious with unbelievers? How can we not be gentle and respectful when we were lost ourselves?[18] As Michaels writes, "this God-centered quality of the heart

---

18. John M. Frame, *Apologetics: A Justification of Christian Belief* (Phillipsburg, NJ.: P&R Publishing, 2015), 29.

finds expression in one's behavior toward others", for whatever happens with the human heart will affect all other relationships that stem from it.[19]

---

19. Michaels, *Word Biblical Commentary, Vol. 49: 1 Peter*, 189.

CHAPTER

3

WHAT IS APOLOGETICS?

IN LIGHT of what the apostle Peter has written in this verse, how are we, therefore, to understand apologetics? The late theologian, Cornelius Van Til, defined apologetics as "the vindication of the Christian philosophy of life against the various forms of the non-Christian philosophy of life".[20] In simpler terms, one of Van Til's students, John M. Frame, a contemporary and prominent theologian and philosopher, defines this as "the discipline that teaches Christians how to give a reason for their hope… precisely the certitude of God's Word," for the truthfulness of God's Word implies the falsity of all things contrary to it.[21]

Apologetics is a multi-faceted discipline. It has many aspects that, for the untrained Christian, can make it appear daunting or intimidating. But with adequate instruction, coupled with a faith firmly rooted in Scripture, apologetics can furnish the Christian with a powerful and effective gospel witness. Frame,

---

20. Cornelius Van Til, *Christian Apologetics*, Second edition. ed. William Edgar (Phillipsburg, NJ.: P&R Publishing, 2003), 17.

21. Frame, *Apologetics*, 1.

in his book *Apologetics*, lists three aspects to apologetics, these are:

(1) Apologetics as proof;
(2) Apologetics as defense;
(3) Apologetics as offense.[22]

In regard to the *first aspect*, apologetics is to be understood as "presenting a rational basis for the Christian faith,"[23] or to put it differently, presenting the Christian religious worldview as the *only* rational worldview. Christians do not believe in an invented reality, in an illusion, they believe in the true interpretation of created reality as provided by God's written revelation. They believe things as they truly are. To elaborate on this matter, Christians believe in the one and only *true* worldview, which can be defined as:

> a network of presuppositions (which are not verified by the procedures of natural science) regarding reality (metaphysics), know-

---

22. Ibid., 1.
23. Ibid.

ing (epistemology), and conduct (ethics) in terms of which every element of human experience is related and interpreted.[24]

Every living person has a worldview, a set of presuppositions concerning reality, ethics, and knowledge. But no worldview is irreligious. A person's worldview can be considered the *structure* of his presuppositions; his religion, however, can be considered the *direction* of his presuppositions, the object that is worshiped. This reality is undeniably evident in the plethora of religions and philosophies that have existed throughout human history. However, just as every *living* person has a religious worldview, every person who has *passed* from this life now knows what the *true* religious worldview is. And for all of those who had rejected the true religious worldview, this realization is far too late for them, for one's religious worldview, not only professed but lived out, determines their

---

24. Gary DeMar, ed., *Pushing the Antithesis: The Apologetic Methodology of Greg L. Bahnsen* (Powder Springs, GA.: American Vision Press, 2010), 42-43.

eternal destination (Matt. 7:13-14). The apologetic task, therefore, involves proving the truthfulness of the Christian religious worldview by demonstrating the impossibility, and thus futility, of the contrary. That is what Van Til meant by "the vindication of the Christian philosophy of life against the various forms of the non-Christian philosophy of life."[25]

In regard to the *second aspect*, apologetics is also to be understood as "answering the objections of unbelief."[26] Consider, for example, Paul's words to the Philippians: "…I hold you in my heart, for you are all partakers with me of grace, both in my imprisonment and *in the defense and confirmation of the gospel*" (Phil. 1:7). By "confirmation", Paul means the vindication of the Christian philosophy of life, but by "defense" he means "giving answers to objections."[27] This is not something that the Christian should avoid. In fact, just as objections are to be expected, so it is likewise

---

25. Van Til, *Christian Apologetics*, 17.

26. Frame, *Apologetics*, 2.

27. Ibid.

expected that the Christian promptly responds to them. Paul, for example, answered his objectors – even objections that he had anticipated might arise amongst those whom he ministered to (cf. Acts 22:1; 24:10; 25:8, 16; 26:1-2, 24). It could be said that he was "always ready."

In regard to the *third aspect*, apologetics is to be understood as "attacking the foolishness of unbelieving thought."[28] To be clear, this is not to be understood as an attack against the unbeliever, this would, after all, contravene Peter's apostolic instruction of responding with gentleness and respect, but rather, to attack the antithetical *philosophy* of life, that all men may be left without excuse before God (Rom. 1:20). Consider what Paul writes: "We destroy arguments and every lofty opinion raised against the knowledge of God, and take every thought captive to obey Christ" (2 Cor. 10:5). The late apologist Greg L. Bahnsen writes, in regard to Paul's words, that:

---

28. Ibid., 2.

believers have the advantage of the best reasoning and philosophy because Christ is the source of all knowledge – *all* knowledge, not simply religious matters or sentiment... Any alleged wisdom which follows the traditions of men and elementary principles of the world – rather than Christ – is to be rejected as dangerous and deceitful... We are not to obscure the glory and veracity of God by answering unbelievers with appeals to "blind faith" or thoughtless commitment. We are to "cast down reasonings and every high thing exalted against the knowledge of God" (2 Cor. 10:5), realizing all along that we cannot do so unless we ourselves "bring every thought captive to the obedience of Christ."[29]

Having laid out these three aspects of (1) proof,

---

29. Greg L. Bahnsen, *Always Ready: Directions for Defending the Faith*, ed., Robert R. Booth (Nacogdoches, TX.: Covenant Media Press, 2011, 114-115.

(2) defense and (3) offense, it may occur to us that there may be some overlap, and this certainly would not be wrong. In fact, these three aspects presuppose and supplement one another. Frame articulates this fact: "To give a full account of the rationale of [Christian] belief (no. 1), one must vindicate that rationale against the objections (no. 2) and alternatives (no. 3) advanced by unbelievers."[30] For how could one possibly argue for the exclusivity of the Christian religious worldview without considering the unbeliever's objections, or the alternatives that are put forward? Of what potency would such an apologetic be? Or of what effectiveness? Apologetics, therefore, is not solely one aspect and not the other, *all three aspects* together reflect the discipline of Christian apologetics.

But there is a prerequisite to doing apologetics, and it is found in what Peter writes in the opening of the fifteenth verse, "But in your hearts honor Christ the Lord as holy." In regard to this text, I had stated above that Christians are to reflect the holiness of Je-

---

30. Ibid.

sus Christ through everything they do, the life expression of their confession that Jesus Christ is Lord. And while external works of righteousness may perhaps be at the forefront of our minds – for what is faith without good works? (Jam. 2:14-26) – what is also being communicated here is that our *thinking* must be made subject to the lordship of Christ, or to put it differently, that our thinking *pays tribute* to Christ's lordship. How so? If we adopt God's Word to be our ultimate starting point for all thinking, our ultimate epistemological authority, or as Frame puts it:

> if we adopt the Word of God as our ultimate commitment, our ultimate standard, our ultimate criterion of truth and falsity, God's Word then becomes our "presupposition." That is to say, since we use it to evaluate all other beliefs, we must regard it as more certain than any other beliefs.[31]

To put it plainly, to adopt the presupposition of God's Word is what results in a manner of thinking

---

31. Frame, *Apologetics: A Justification of Christian Belief.*

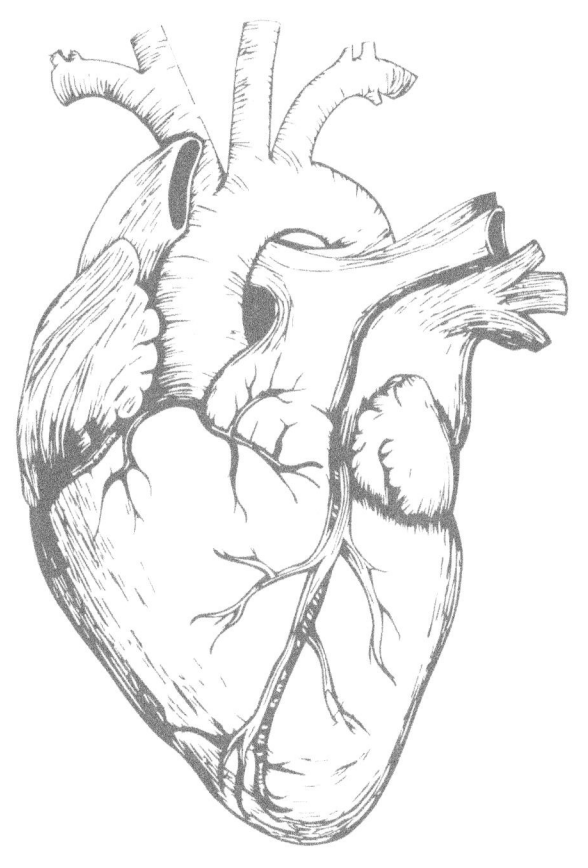

that honours Christ's lordship, and this can only be done if the person's heart has been regenerated by the Spirit of God (cf. Rom. 10:9; 1 Cor. 12:3; Phil. 2:11).[32] For how can we honour Christ in our thinking if our root unity, our hearts, do not honour God? We need to be grace-redeemed believers committed to the lordship of Christ; that must be our ultimate presupposition, our basic-heart commitment, our ultimate trust.[33]

This reverence is also emphasized by Grudem, who states that

> the phrase [*hagiázō*] is also an adaptation of part of Isaiah 8:13, "But the LORD of hosts, him you shall regard as holy; let him be your fear, and let him be your dread." Thus the sense of fear or reverence for the Lord rather than fear of men is reinforced.[34]

---

32. Ibid.

33. Ibid., 6.

34. Grudem, *Tyndale New Testament Commentaries: 1 Peter*, 160.

The Christian's allegiance, therefore – including in the area of his thought – is to Christ, the One through whom all things were made (Jn. 1:3; Col. 1:16), and who reigns with all power over creation (Matt. 28:18; 1 Cor. 15:25). He calls us to *absolute* loyalty, and instructs us to prohibit anything that could compete with that loyalty (Deut. 6:4ff; Matt. 6:24; 12:30; Jn. 14:6; Acts 4:12). This loyalty, this basic-heart commitment, this ultimate presupposition, is in stark contrast to the sin-induced hostility of the natural man who stumbles in the dark, vainly attempting to invent his own reality from his pretended autonomy (Rom. 1:18). To be an apologist, to do apologetics, and to fulfill the apologetic mandate, you must first honour "Christ the Lord as holy…" (1 Pet. 3:15a), for this sets us apart from the world's way of living and thinking. This ultimate presupposition is in fact the prerequisite for Christian apologetics.

CHAPTER 4

A HOLISTIC FAITH

HOWEVER, WHILE Frame excellently lays out the three aspects of the discipline of apologetics, there is still more to be said regarding the territory that apologetics covers. Given that the Christian religious worldview is not a 'private' faith by any stretch, being solely concerned with the spiritual life of the individual, but is rather all-comprehensive and all-encompassing, in the same way, apologetics has an all-comprehensive and all-encompassing scope.

This holistic nature of apologetics can be demonstrated in how it is employed. Van Til, for example, in his book *Christian Apologetics*, makes the distinction between the evidential and the philosophical, and by this he does not mean the evidential and classical methods or approach, but rather, that apologetics can be employed for both evidential and philosophical argumentation.[35] According to Van Til, the evidential largely deals with the historical, but apologetics is not confined solely to the historical, it is far more expansive than that, dealing most predominantly with

---

35. Van Til, *Christian Apologetics*, 19.

the philosophical. How to best illustrate this? While evidential (also referred to as 'factual') argumentation can be necessary at times, such a discussion cannot yet take place until the underlying philosophy of evidences and facts are first addressed. An atheist, for example, may want to build his argument for human origins on the historic find of "Lucy the hominid", but prior to discussing that piece of evidence, a conversation must be had as to what *is* evidence, how evidence could be *intelligible* to the human mind, and how we might *know* that we are rightly interpreting the evidence.[36] As Van Til writes:

> To interpret a fact of history involves a philosophy of history. But a philosophy of history is at the same time a philosophy of reality as a whole. Thus we are driven to philosophical discussion all the time and everywhere.[37]

---

36. See Marvin L. Lubenow, *Bones of Contention: A Creationist Assessment of Human Fossils* (Grand Rapids, MI.: Baker Books, 2007).

37. Ibid.

And if we are driven to "philosophical discussion all the time and everywhere", and philosophy can be defined as the "discipline of the disciplines", then we must understand the scope of apologetics to be all-comprehensive.[38] And that means that, while we can certainly engage on specifics, such as evidential argumentation, Christianity can "never be separated from some theory about the existence and the nature of God", or to put it more simply, we cannot break the Christian religious worldview into multiple independent components when it is truthfully a *whole* unit.[39] To communicate this concept of the holism of Christian theism, Van Til provides a military illustration on the versatility and adaptability of Christian apologetics:

> We may... compare the vindication of Christian theism *as a whole* to modern warfare.

---

38. For more on philosophy as the discipline of the disciplines, see D.F.M. Strauss, *Philosophy: Discipline of the Disciplines* (Jordan Station, ON.: Paideia Press, 2009).

39. Van Til, *Christian Apologetics*, 18.

> There is bayonet fighting, there is rifle shooting, there are machine guns, but there are also heavy cannon and atom bombs. All the men engaged in these different kinds of fighting are mutually dependent upon one another. The rifle men could do very little if they did not fight under the protection of the heavy guns behind them. The heavy guns depend for the progress they make upon the smaller guns. So too with Christian theism. It is impossible and useless to seek to vindicate Christianity as a historical religion by a discussion of facts only.[40]

This holistic understanding of the faith is precisely what Peter had in mind, for as Grudem affirms, "To have such reverence *in your hearts* is to maintain continually a deep-seated inward confidence in Christ as reigning Lord and King, who even now has 'angels, authorities, and powers subject to him' (3:22)."[41] In

---

40. Ibid.
41. Grudem, *Tyndale New Testament Commentaries: 1 Peter*, 160.

other words, we must honour Christ as Lord over *all* creation, and therefore our faith, our apologetic, must be all-encompassing in its scope, a reflection of a comprehensive and holistic worldview.

How could our apologetic *not* be holistic and comprehensive when Christ is Lord over all creation? As the text of 1 Corinthians 15:27 reads: "For 'God has put all things in subjection under his feet.'" Is there anything in created reality that is not under Christ's dominion? Of course not. Why then should we think that apologetics applies only to spiritual or historical matters as the forces of secularism and Christian privatism would like us to think? The Christian religious worldview does in fact have much to say about government, politics, ethics, education, the arts, and anything else you could possibly imagine. There really is no such thing as a public and a private sphere, or an ecclesiastical and a common kingdom, *all* of created reality is under the domain of Christ's lordship.

And because of this all-encompassing domain, His authoritative Scriptural revelation is, as a result, relevant for and applicable to all aspects of life. As Van Til explains:

> The Bible is at the center... it speaks of everything. We do not mean that it speaks of football games, of atoms, etc., directly, but we do mean that it speaks of everything either directly or by implication. It not only tells us of the Christ and his work, but also tells us who God is and where the universe about us has come from. It tells us about theism as well as about Christianity. It gives us a philosophy of history as well as history. Moreover, the information on these subjects is woven into an inextricable whole.[42]

The Christian does not, therefore, ascribe to a privatized Christianity, some pious spirituality divorced from the rest of reality. The Christian instead holds to a comprehensive, all-encompassing faith, a religious *world-and-life* view, a *philosophy of life*. To posit otherwise would be to reject the Bible as God's Word, in

---
42. Van Til, *Christian Apologetics*, 19-20.

fact, it would be to reject the God of Christian theism, for as Van Til rightly states, "there is nothing in this universe on which human beings can have full and true information unless they take the Bible into account."[43]

---

43. Ibid., 20.

CHAPTER 5

THE NATURE OF APOLOGETICS

THIS COMPREHENSIVENESS of the faith, however, has largely been lost in recent times due to its increased privatization, producing nothing more than a caricature of biblical Christianity. As a result, the mission of the church has also been skewed to something that it is not. In fact, in the past few decades, the mission of the church has characteristically become more defensive and retreatist than offensive and triumphant. Charles H. Spurgeon, the prince of preachers of the late nineteenth century, would have disagreed with the defensive missiological posture reflected by most of the church today, that is not after all how he had understood Jesus' description of the church as being the "salt and light of the world." Spurgeon's commentary is consulted further below. But before considering his writing, it must be stated that Grudem also, when writing on 1 Peter 3:15 and its contextual understanding, rightly identifies the Bible's description of the missiological nature of the church as being forward-moving and outward-turned. Grudem writes that:

the stance of Christians toward unbelievers must never be merely passive or neutral... [Peter] goes on to encourage preparation for active witness which will win the unbeliever to Christ... Paul provides a good example of seizing the offensive and bearing testimony to Christ even when on trial himself (Acts 22:1-21; 24:10-24; 26:1-23, 25b-29). In hostile situations the opportunity for witness to Christ often comes unexpectedly; the Christian who is not always ready to answer will miss it.[44]

In order to best understand the nature of apologetics, recognizing what the apologetic mandate entails, we can turn to Jesus' teaching of the church as being the "light" and "salt" of the earth. Consider what He says in His sermon on the mount:

"You are the salt of the earth, but if salt has lost its taste, how shall its saltiness be re-

---

44. Grudem, *Tyndale New Testament Commentaries: 1 Peter*, 161.

stored? It is no longer good for anything except to be thrown out and trampled under people's feet. You are the light of the world. A city set on a hill cannot be hidden. Nor do people light a lamp and put it under a basket, but on a stand, and it gives light to all in the house. In the same way, let your light shine before others, so that they may see your good works and give glory to your Father who is in heaven..." (Matt. 5:13-16).

How might this relate to the nature of apologetics? How does this establish the *modus operandi* for the apologetic mandate? Before these questions can be answered, consider what Spurgeon has to say on this respective passage:

> In [the church] there is a preserving force to keep the rest of society from utter corruption. If [the church] were not scattered among men, the race would putrefy... We are to remove the darkness of ignorance, sin, and sorrow. Christ has lighted us that we

> may enlighten the world... God intends his grace to be as conspicuous as a city built on the mountain's brow.[45]

What Spurgeon provides us with in his typical delectable writing is the nature of the application of Jesus' teaching, which should make the connection, or relevance of this passage to the missiological nature of apologetics more apparent. To elaborate: the apologetic mandate entails two aspects in regard to its *modus operandi* (its operational method), that of (i) preserving, and that of (ii) advancing – these two are inseparably tied to the church's gospel witness.

How so? The church is called to be the salt of the earth, this means that, as the gospel is proclaimed, and as the teaching of the Word of God is wisely applied to all areas of life, there should be a *regression* of the

---

45. Charles H. Spurgeon, *The Gospel of the Kingdom: A Popular Exposition of the Gospel according to Matthew* (New York, NY.: The Baker & Taylor Co., 1893), 45-46.; "Putrefy" means "decay or rot and produce a fetid smell" according to Oxford Languages, *Lexico*. Accessed June 6, 2020, https://www.lexico.com/en/definition/putrefy/.

darkness and depravity brought about by the sinfulness of humanity. Consider, for example, the thousands upon thousands of human sacrifices offered up to false idols by the ancient civilizations of the Aztecs, Incas and Nazca, to name a few. If it were not for the cultural fruits of a holistic Christianity, such practices would have continued for who knows how many more centuries. While historically there are many factors to consider, and I do risk oversimplifying this transitional process that took place in Ibero-America, it is nonetheless indisputable that the departure from a culture of death was chiefly the result of an introduction of a culture marked by the life and light of the gospel.[46] Sorrowfully, with the departure from historic Christendom and the increased privatization of the Christian faith, human sacrifices have been re-

---

46. The gospel distortion of Roman Catholicism and the corruption of the Spanish Empire during the period of New World colonization are both well documented, however, the following has still proven true: God can still accomplish far more than man can think or imagine, even with a small sliver of light (Eph. 3:20).

ALWAYS READY

turning to the West in the forms of medical abortion and euthanasia. And the aforementioned regression of darkness and depravity is now experiencing a full-blown resurgence and progression. The Indian philosopher Vishal Mangalwadi, author of *The Book that Made Your World*, wisely cites George Orwell in relation to how we can understand what has happened in the Western world:

> For two hundred years we had sawed and sawed and sawed at the branch we were sitting on. And in the end, much more suddenly than anyone had foreseen, our efforts were rewarded, and down we came. But unfortunately there had been a little mistake: The thing at the bottom was not a bed of roses after all; it was a cesspool full of barbed wire... It appears that amputation of the soul isn't just a simple surgical job, like having your appendix out. The wound has a tendency to go septic.[47]

---

47. "George Orwell, Notes on the Way, 1940" cited in Vishal

Given our current reality, and the inevitable consequence of departing from the Christian religious worldview at a personal and cultural level, it is all the more important that the apologetic offered by the church be reformed to the faithful teaching of Scripture, and this entails preserving the truth, beauty, and goodness of God's creation through the proclamation of the gospel and the universal application of God's Word; for its effects are far reaching – impacting first the individual, followed by the family, the community, the academy and the socio-cultural order. To put it plainly, Christian apologetics must function in the manner of *preservation* if it is to be in line with the missional identity and purpose of the church.

But the work of preservation alone is insufficient. The church is not just called to keep back the darkness of this world, it is also called to be the light of the earth. This means that the gospel that proclaims the Christian philosophy of life is to go forth to all the

---

Mangalwadi, *The Book that Made Your World: How the Bible Created the Soul of Western Civilization* (Nashville, TN.: Thomas Nelson, 2011), 3.

four corners of the world, to every sphere of society, to every aspect of culture, for in doing so, it not only brings everything that was dark and murky (corrupt and evil) into the clear light to be judged, it brings about the vanquishing of the darkness. How so? The fourth century bishop St. Athanasius writes that through the gospel work of the church:

> the Saviour works mightily every day, drawing men to [true] religion, persuading them to virtue, teaching them about immortality, quickening their thirst for heavenly things, revealing the knowledge of the Father, inspiring strength in the face of death, manifesting Himself to each, and displacing the irreligion of idols; while the gods and evil spirits of the unbelievers can do none of these things, but rather become dead at Christ's presence, all their ostentation barren and void. By the sign of the cross, on the contrary, all magic is stayed, all sorcery confounded, all the idols are abandoned and

deserted, and all senseless pleasure ceases as the eye of faith looks up from earth to heaven.[48]

In more modern terms, the scholar David Chilton explains the "advancement" aspect of the church, as laid out by Matthew 5:13-16, in the introduction to his book *Paradise Restored*. Whereas Athanasius highlighted the work of Christ through the work of the church, Chilton elaborates as to what the work of the church entails:

> This [passage] is nothing less than a mandate for the complete social transformation of the entire world. And what Jesus condemns is *ineffectiveness*, failing to change the society around us. We are commanded to live in such a way that someday all men

---

48. St. Athanasius, "On the Incarnation" in *A Celebration of Faith Series: Defender of Orthodox Christology | On the Incarnation*, ed., Steven R. Martins, trans., Philip Schaff (Jordan Station, ON.: Cántaro Publications, 2020), 110-111.

will glorify God – that they will become converted to the Christian faith. The point is that if the Church is obedient, the people and nations of the world will be discipled to Christianity. We all know that everyone *should* be a Christian, that the laws and institutions of all nations *should* follow the Bible's blueprints. But the Bible tells us more than that. The Bible tells us that these commands are the shape of the future. We *must* change the world; and what is more, we *shall* change the world.[49]

Just as Christian apologetics must function in the manner of *preservation* in order to be in line with the missional identity and the purpose of the church, so it must also function in the manner of *advancement*. In fact, these two aspects of (i) preserving and (ii) advancing presuppose and supplement one another. For how can there be any preservation of truth, beauty,

---

49. David Chilton, *Paradise Restored: An Eschatology of Dominion* (Tyler, TX.: Reconstruction Press, 1985), 12.

and goodness if there is no advancement of the Christian philosophy of life? And how can there be any advancement of the Christian philosophy of life, if there is no preservation of that which is true, beautiful, and good?

Understanding the missiological nature of the church enables us to reconcile these two aforementioned aspects, that being (i) preservation and (ii) advancement, with what Van Til and Frame had laid out. The truth is that there really is not anything to "reconcile". On the contrary, what we should have is a fuller and clearer picture of the apologetic mandate, along with solid biblical warrant for what has been previously articulated. The apologetic mandate is, essentially, *the vindication of the Christian philosophy of life over all non-Christian philosophies of life,* it involves *presenting a rational basis for the Christian religious worldview, answering the objections of unbelief, and destroying all alternative unbelieving (anti-Christian) thought systems to the glory of God alone.*

CHAPTER 6

CONCLUDING REMARKS

CHRISTIAN APOLOGETICS is not, therefore, a discipline confined to evidential argumentation, whether it be concerning the historicity of Jesus, the age of the Earth, or the textual fidelity of the Scriptures; it is, in contrast, a discipline that addresses every aspect of man's creational interaction – think the academy, the market, the church, the family, the state, and society. Scripture has much to say regarding all these spheres, but unfortunately, the church has largely remained silent because of the faith's increasing privatization. The apologetic mandate, however, cannot be relegated to the periphery by today's privatized 'Christianity'. On the contrary, the apologetic mandate is all-encompassing in its nature and scope according to the clear teaching of Scripture. It cannot *not* be when we consider the undeniable comprehensiveness of a person's worldview, and the clear cosmic scope of the gospel. Biblical Christianity is a *world-and-life view*, it is THE world-and-life view, nothing less.

Peter's apostolic instruction to the collective church extends well beyond his own time: the church is to always be ready to provide an answer, an *apologia*, for the hope of Christ within us. May we press on towards preserving the truth, beauty, and goodness of God's creation and advancing the Christian philosophy of life by the proclamation of the gospel and the wise application of his Scriptural revelation. Paul stood at the ready, as did the rest of the apostles, as did the church fathers, many of whom were martyred, and as did the Christian church for most of its history – may we be ready and found faithful to our Lord Jesus Christ, for in this fallen world, we will always be placed on trial, until the day when Christ puts all things in subjection to Himself:

> Then comes the end, when he delivers the kingdom to God the Father after destroying every rule and every authority and power. For he must reign until he has put all his enemies under his feet. The last enemy to be destroyed is death. For "God has put all things in subjection under his feet." But when it says, "all things are put in subjec-

CONCLUDING REMARKS

tion," it is plain that he is excepted who put all things in subjection under him. When all things are subjected to him, then the Son himself will also be subjected to him who put all things in subjection under him, that God may be all in all. (1 Cor. 15:24-28).

SCRIPTURE INDEX

Deuteronomy		24:10	27, 42
6:4	50	24:10-24	68
Psalm		25:8	27, 42
102:25-26	31	25:16	27, 42
Isaiah		26:1-2	27, 42
11:6-9	31	26:1-23	68
25:8	31	26:24	27, 42
65:17	31	26:25-29	68
Matthew		**Romans**	
5:5	33	1:18	50
5:13-16	70	1:20	43
6:9	24	8:22-24	31
6:24	50	10:9	48
7:13-14	40	**1 Corinthians**	
12:30	50	12:3	48
28:18	50	15:24-28	87-88
28:18-20	15	15:25	50
John		15:26	31
1:3	50	15:27	61
14:6	50	15:54	31
Acts		**2 Corinthians**	
4:12	50	2:11	27
22:1	27, 42	10:5	43, 44
22:1-21	68		

SCRIPTURE INDEX

Galatians	
5:22-23	21

Ephesians	
3:20	73

Philippians	
1:7	27, 41
1:16	27
2:11	48

Colossians	
1:16	50

2 Timothy	
4:16	27

James	
2:14-26	47

1 Peter	
1:1-2	19
1:15-16	26
1:18	20
1:21	20
2:6	20
2:9	20, 26
2:11-12	20
3:3-4	31
3:8-22	21
3:15	16, 20, 27, 50
3:22	61
4:3-5	20
5:13	20

2 Peter	
3:10-13	31

Revelation	
21	31

ABOUT THE AUTHOR

STEVEN R. MARTINS is a Christian thinker and writer, founding director of the Cántaro Institute and founding pastor of Sevilla Chapel in St. Catharines, ON. He has worked in the fields of missional apologetics and church leadership for ten years and has spoken at numerous conferences, churches, and University student events. He has also contributed articles to *Coalición por el Evangelio* (TGC in Spanish) and the *Siglo XXI* journal of Editorial CLIR. Steven holds a Master's degree *summa cum laude* in Theological Studies with a focus on Christian apologetics from Veritas International University (Santa Ana, CA., USA) and a Bachelor of Human Resource Management from York University (Toronto, ON., Canada). Steven is married to Cindy and they live in Lincoln, Ontario, with their sons Matthias, Timothy, and Nehemías.